The Great Teenage Myth

Stop Living That Darn Lie!

by Joseph P. Gandolfo

New York

The Great Teenage Myth

Stop Living That Darn Lie!

ISBN 978-1-60037-618-4

Library of Congress Control Number: 2009924312

MORGAN · JAMES
THE ENTREPRENEURIAL PUBLISHER

Morgan James Publishing, LLC
1225 Franklin Ave., STE 325
Garden City, NY 11530-1693
Toll Free 800-485-4943
www.MorganJamesPublishing.com

In an effort to support local communities, raise awareness and funds, Morgan James Publishing donates one percent of all book sales for the life of each book to Habitat for Humanity. Get involved today, visit **www.HelpHabitatForHumanity.org.**

Dedication

*To Tonya, Cole, Duncan
and
My Italian Family*

Table of Contents

Foreword

The teenage years can be a turbulent time for a young person as you solidify your personality, ambition, and life goals. Gandolfo has taken a brilliant look at how teenagers can attain their dreams by overcoming the myths that are often applied to their age group.

I have witnessed magnificent transitions of thousands of our students at High Point University where I serve as president. I teach a required course to all freshmen and seniors on life skills and developing positive life habits. When students submit their personal essays throughout the course of the semester, I have realized that young people are far more brilliant than they receive credit for by the world.

Gandolfo's book is a must for understanding how to reach your goals efficiently and impress the world with your talents. Study this book and benefit from the expertise and experience he outlines. Apply relevant concepts to your life, and prepare your mind for what lies ahead.

Nido Qubein
President, High Point University
Chairman, Great Harvest Bread Company

The

Great Teenage Myth

Is there anybody … *listening?*

Is there anybody …
out there?

Joe Gandolfo

What is that?

A dot or a spot?

Is it a black dot ...
on a white page?

Or is it a white page ... with a spot on it?

*Do you ever feel
this small?*

Do you ever feel so

Big

that everything in life seems this

small?

*Do you ever feel all
alone?*

*Do you feel like your life
is standing still
stagnating —
and not going anywhere?*

Is your life not what you have wished for?

*Have you ever wanted
to be
far, far away?*

Let's play *"what if"* –
what if you were really
far away, so far away that you were
out in space?

This is what the earth
might look like from
far, far away.

Consider this truth. If you were as far away from the earth as the moon, which is about 238,857 miles, this is how the earth—**YOUR WORLD**—would look.

A planet, the Earth,
YOUR WORLD,
OUR WORLD.

Now, if you flew down and landed on this big rock we call Earth, which is spinning at approximately 1,040 miles per hour and hurtling through space, orbiting the sun at approximately 67,000 miles per hour ...

... logic would say that you would go flying off **OUR WORLD**, right? But here you are, *connected to* the Earth and not flying off no matter how fast our world is spinning.

And, as you walk through your day, it doesn't even feel like the ground is moving ... *does it?*

So what you perceive as true isn't always true ... is it? Sometimes, what appears to be real—**true**—isn't actually real—**true.**

The Gift All Humans Have

As human beings, we are blessed with the ability—the gift—of being able to *change* **our perceptions** and **our point of view.**

Here's an example:

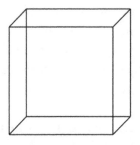

Look at the box above. Can you shift your eyes from the front of the box to the back of the box? First, you see the front of the box. Now, you see the back of the box. The <u>front</u> of the box **becomes** the <u>back</u> of the box, and the <u>back</u> of the box **becomes** the <u>front</u> of the box.

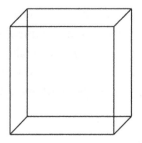

Is it your eyes that make the box *shift?* NO! Your eyes simply look at the one-dimensional drawing of the box. It's your brain—**your mind**—that has to shift your perception, **your point of view.**

Once your mind *allows* this shift to happen, you see the box in a **TOTALLY DIFFERENT WAY!**

Your pets can't do this! No other animal, insect, reptile, fish, or bird can do this! Understand, NO other living creature can do this!

Know that ONLY humans have the ability to THINK and take a new idea—a different perspective or point of view—and roll that new idea around in *their minds* thus being able to make a decision regarding the *usefulness* or *uselessness* of that new idea if it were applied and integrated into their lives.

Only human beings can do this! It's an **amazingly powerful gift** you can use in your life! You've heard about "thinking outside the box," right? When you *shift,* and thus expand your perceptions, you move your thinking out of "a box"—a paradigm—and give your mind the freedom to THINK and **consider something new and different.**

It's All About Awareness!

The results in your life are directly related to how you look at things, how much you understand, your level of awareness, the effort you put forth, and the action you take. The more awareness you have about your life, the greater opportunity you will have to be able to make the changes that will make your life better.

Did you know...

- While sitting in a chair on this earth, your speed is 1.9 million miles per hour! *(Things are not always as they appear.)*

- Side by side, 2,000 cells from the human body would cover about one square inch! *(Your body is a living miracle!)*

- Your body uses 300 muscles to balance itself when you're standing still! *(Your body is amazing!)*

- Humans share one-third of their DNA with lettuce! *(Everything on our Earth is made of the same stuff!)*

- The Earth is hit by lightning 100 times a second! *(There is more energy and power in you than you can imagine!)*

- Sixty-five people become millionaires every day! *(Ideas, opportunities, and abundance are all around you!)*

- Every person in the U.S. produces 1,609 pounds of garbage each year! *(Waste! What are you wasting in your life?)*

I share these interesting facts to begin to shake up your mind, to loosen up your current perceptions, to challenge your current point of view, and to get you to begin to **THINK!**

I want you to consider *the* opportunity, YOUR opportunity, to shatter *The Great Teenage Myth*, because this *MYTH* has you shackled and confined like a prisoner. **YES, like a prisoner!**

But you don't have to be a prisoner any longer. **You CAN have more of what you want!**

So What Do ALL Teenagers Want?

I have asked thousands of teenagers this simple question: *What do you want to have in your life?*

Many of the answers have been: *I want a car. I want more money. I want more stuff—computers, computer games, video games, electronics, toys. I want more clothes.*

Some teenagers want later curfews, more privacy in their bedrooms, their own place to live, or a say in the decisions of their lives. Some want to travel; others want to start a company. Many teenagers—deep inside—want to do better in school.

Believe it or not, many teens want a deeper connection with their parents, even if they don't believe it can happen or are at a loss about how to make it happen.

The list of answers to this question goes on and on.

But I have found that, when teens take a THINKING exploration of all of these *wants,* drilling down deep inside, what they really, really want are:

More Freedom!
More Independence!

More Personal Power!
Fewer Hassles!

Think about it a minute.

Aren't these the things you truly want?

Only if you are willing to understand, consider, and shatter *The Great Teenage Myth* will you have given yourself the opportunity to experience and live what you truly desire and need in your life: **Real Freedom, Real Independence,** and **Real Personal Power!!**

As one of today's teenagers, you unknowingly believe in—and are living—one of the greatest, most deceptive, most destructive *MYTHS* in the world.

You are not only <u>living</u> *The Great Teenage Myth*, you are perpetuating it each and every day, keeping its destructive power alive by sharing it with your friends and classmates.

You keep *The Great Teenage Myth* alive and even strengthen it wherever you gather and interact with other teens: in your classrooms and school hallways, at ball games, in your neighborhoods, in your backyards, in the basements where you hang out, or through your text messages and online social networks.

Does that surprise you?
Are you puzzled?

What may be even more surprising is that back when they were teenagers, most of your parents bought into and perpetuated the *MYTH* too. Some adults still believe it and live the *MYTH* to this day! I certainly lived the *MYTH* when I was younger, long before I personally shattered the *MYTH* in my early twenties. *The Great Teenage Myth* has been believed and handed down for generations.

Although most myths are harmless, this one is destructive.

It's destructive in the world and, more important, incredibly destructive to **you personally.** It prevents you from having in your life what you most **DESIRE, WANT,** and **NEED—Real Freedom, Real Independence, Real Personal Power,** and **Fewer Hassles!**

The Great Teenage Myth is so powerful in fact that some people are trapped in it their whole lives. But you can be free of it.

CURIOUS?

Read on!

The

Great Teenage Myth

The Origins of The Great Teenage Myth

Okay, I know you want to know the *MYTH* right now. But first I want to shake up your mind a little more. Some of this information may blow your mind! But it's important for you to understand how *The Great Teenage Myth* came into being. Then you'll see it for what it is – a *misperception* – a faulty idea and concept that you can let go of *if* you are willing and open to *shifting* your point of view!

Key Point #1

The whole idea of "play" as teenagers' experience it today **is a relatively new concept.** The manner in which you play, the manner in which your parents played, the manner in which I played, and the manner in which my kids play is something that has only been going on for the last six or seven decades (since the late 1940s)!

Key Point #2

Before 1940, just over 65 years ago, **there was technically no such thing as a teenager.** The word "teenager" and the experience of "teen life" did not exist at all; it is truly a new phenomenon. Over the course of human history, maturity (or adulthood), was measured on the basis of physical size and capability, not age.

The Hunters and Gathers

Until about 10,000 years ago, all human beings were hunters and gatherers. That means they fed themselves by hunting game (maybe fishing if they lived near water) and picking fruits and other plants they found in the wild. Even little kids were expected to help with the food gathering, which was mostly women's work.

The men and boys who were big enough did the hunting, usually for small rodents, and spent the rest of their time making primitive tools or weapons.

The women and girls prepared the food and took care of the little ones who weren't old enough to walk or do chores themselves. They also made the clothes and tents and did the packing and unpacking every time the clan moved. That was pretty often, unless the tribe was lucky enough to live in a mild climate with plenty of edible plants and year-round game.

Simple survival took up so much of each day that there wasn't much time for play. And, after nightfall, it was too dark ... not to mention dangerous.

To get an idea of what it might have been like to live back then, close your eyes and imagine yourself sitting in your current bedroom. Take a minute to get a clear mental picture of your surroundings. **Got it?**

Now start subtracting everything you see that runs on electricity or batteries: your TV, VCR, DVD player, computer, Nintendo games, play stations and Xbox, your CD player, cell phone, iPod! Don't forget the lights, air conditioning and heat.

Now get rid of everything made of paper, plastic, metal, glass, concrete, brick, synthetic fabrics, even cotton and wool (hunter-gatherers didn't farm or herd sheep). Right about now, you may be looking for a leafy bush or large rock to hide behind. Not only do you have no playthings or "stuff," but you're out in the open without any clothes on!

By the way, you wouldn't have had your own room either. Whole families usually lived in a single space, like a cave or animal-skin tent that could be quickly put up and taken down when the tribe moved on.

Because survival was such a huge part of everyday life, educational activities tended to center around learning how to identify nonpoisonous plants and how to track and kill game. Not learning your lessons at an early age could literally be a matter of life or death. There were no stores or money so, aside from food, you had to make anything you wanted or create something that you could trade with someone else.

Everyone created their own music and did the same dances, which were typically performed to appease the gods. And for entertainment, instead of spending evenings in front of the TV or computer, families sat around an open fire telling stories.

IMPORTANT UNDERSTANDING:

"Play"
was a tiny fraction, if any,
of the daily life of
our ancestors.

Agricultural Societies

Let's fast forward a bit and see what life was like for young people after humans started domesticating animals and farming. Once they started growing their own food, people began to settle in one place for longer periods of time. They built more permanent homes of mud or brick, and they began to form communities.

With plenty to eat, more children survived, and families grew bigger. Bigger families were, in fact, a necessity; because farming required a lot more labor than hunting and gathering.

By the time girls were 6 or 7, instead of playing with dolls, they were taking care of real babies: their younger siblings. They were also expected to help with food preparation, spin thread, work in the garden, and tend to the animals. Boys also tended the animals, cut down trees, tilled the soil, planted the crops, helped with the harvest, and performed whatever other heavy labor was required—while still hunting for game.

As populations grew, people did begin to need and want "stuff." At first it was things like big pots for storing extra food or tools for grinding crops into grain. But eventually, the demand for these and other products allowed some of the men to become full-time craftsmen or traders. Sons labored in the family workshop learning their father's craft, or were apprenticed to another man who could teach them a different trade.

No one past the age of 6 was allowed a free ride; young people worked for their keep. And whatever pay they earned outside the home until they reached the age of 21, or were old enough to start their own households, belonged to their parents.

When young people weren't working, their play activities were the same as the adults. Everyone attended the local dances, which were often religious rituals. And a good harvest resulted in feasting for all – from children to grandparents.

Later, agricultural societies in the U.S. had church socials, quilting bees, barn dances and county fairs. The point is that people in their teens didn't spend much time hanging out or doing things together away from adults.

I can hear your next question: What about school? Bear in mind that farming cultures have been around since the Old Testament. The very earliest ones didn't even have written language. As they developed, though, these societies created armies and churches and forms of government that gave people more career choices than farming.

Boys might have started military training or religious studies as early as age 10. But those were career paths that could mean leaving home altogether. Girls weren't sent to school at all since everything they needed to know as wives and mothers could be learned at home.

The early Puritan settlers of North America made sure their children had religious instruction and learned to read. Their sons might also be taught writing and arithmetic. But work was always the top priority, so boys were sent to school in midwinter when there was less to do on the farm.

That's why you hear stories about older generations trudging miles through the snow to a one-room schoolhouse with only a pot-bellied stove for heat. An 18-year-old might even use the same textbook and study the same lessons as an 8-year-old, depending on when he started school and how often he had been able to attend.

The only real energy source in colonial America was the muscle power of its men and animals. "Stuff" was made pretty much the same way it had been for thousands of years. But big changes were in store for everyone, especially young teen women, when textile mills started using water-powered spinning machines.

The Industrial Era (Years)

The industrial age began with the use of machines to make and do things. Machines like the steam engine, spinning jenny, cotton gin, threshing machine, circular saw, and even the first flushing toilet made their appearance. When technology was first brought from Europe to America in the late 1700s, most people lived in rural communities. Lots of young men were sent to cities to learn a trade or profession, but families kept their unmarried daughters at home.

One of the things these young women did well was spin thread. (A "spinster," in fact, was a woman past the marrying age who made her living spinning.) So it made perfect sense that the textile industry started recruiting them off the farm to work in their factories. For a change, a teenage girl could be more valuable to her family as a wage earner than as an extra set of hands around the house.

Factory girls worked up to 14 hours a day, 6 days a week, and they lived in cramped boarding houses provided by the mills. On Sundays, they went to church. For the first time, though, *they were on their own away from home and living with other girls their age.* They also had a little money to spend on "stuff" for themselves. Life in the city offered night courses, libraries, lectures and concerts for those who weren't too exhausted at the end of the day to improve their minds.

Young girls weren't the only ones moving into American cities to take factory jobs, though.

Farming wasn't profitable for everyone, especially those who had only a little land and not much money. When hard times hit, whole families packed up and moved to the city to find work.

Some manufacturers actually preferred having the father, mother and children all working for them.

European immigrants who couldn't find work or support themselves in their countries came to America where jobs were more plentiful. Some of those families took advantage of the new technology to set up their own small-scale manufacturing facilities to make specialized products.

Now that "stuff" was being made, and more people were working outside the home, we began to see the early stages of consumerism.

This was the first time people began to buy "stuff" whether they needed it or not.

After we entered World War I in 1917, there were plenty of jobs for a while with better hours and pay. *Young people kept up with the national news and began to set their own styles.*

It was during the 1920s that people in their late teens began to do their *own* thing. They may have worked with adults, but they hung out and "played" with people their own age.

Then the stock market crash of 1929 hit, followed by the Great Depression, which threw most of the country out of work. In order to give the few available jobs to heads of families, Congress finally passed a law restricting the use of child labor. So, just when young people were starting to have a culture of their own, they suddenly had no money to keep it up.

Since they couldn't work, more teens started going to school on the 5-day schedule we have today. This was the beginning of public school as you know it. By 1940, the vast majority of teenagers were attending public middle and high school.

Before teenage boys and girls started going to school together, parents pretty much controlled who they spent time with. But widespread public middle and high school attendance gave young men and women a peer group outside their families and the chance to get away from parental supervision.

This is the first significant "herding" of preteens and teens in human history.

IMPORTANT UNDERSTANDING:
*It has not been very long
in human history that
"Play"
has been more important
than work in daily
teen life.*

The Age of Consumerism

What finished pulling the U.S. out of the Great Depression was World War II. Both men and women served in the armed forces, and the demand for goods to support the war effort put more people – especially women – to work here at home.

Then, after the war, Congress passed the G.I. Bill, which paid for veterans to go to college and buy houses. People felt optimistic about the future, so they married younger and had more children.

Returning soldiers found better-paying opportunities in urban areas than on the farm. Instead of moving to the inner city, though, they bought houses with backyards in one of the new suburbs on the edge of town. Newlyweds who had grown up in the city moved to the suburbs too, which were, at that time, still pretty close to the cities. And they started buying "stuff" to furnish their new houses.

Machines were developed that could mass-produce goods, and the combination of this with higher wages made more things affordable for these parents of the baby-boom generation.

During the war, people had gone without a lot of life's luxuries, but suddenly they were able to make up for lost time. Soon many households had a refrigerator, washer and dryer, electric toaster, TV, car and telephone. (The phone was usually a "party line," shared with several other families in the neighborhood. In fact, you had to wait until your neighbor finished with the phone before you could "dial" out.)

Parents started buying more "stuff" for their kids too: roller skates, wagons and bicycles, pop guns and Slinky toys, View-Master 3-D viewers and 45-rpm record players, Etch-a-Sketch and hula hoops, Mr. Potato Head and Silly Putty.

One HUGE difference was that many of these parents didn't need for their children to work to help pay the bills. In fact, they *wanted* their kids to stay in school and even go to college to have a more secure future.

IMPORTANT UNDERSTANDING:

*It was during the
1950's when
The
Great Teenage Myth
emerged and began
to take hold.*

The TV Generations

During the late 1940s and early 1950s, houses usually had only one TV. (The number of TVs in American homes grew from about 6 *thousand* in 1945 to an estimated 6 *million* by 1955.)

The two or three channels you might be able to pick up back then – with a "rabbit-ears" antenna on top of the TV set – ran mostly family shows in black and white, which parents and kids watched together.

There was no cable TV, no Cartoon Network, no MTV, no VH1, no ESPN Sports Center, no Disney Channel and no remote control! And sometimes, especially late at night, there was nothing on TV at all but a test pattern like this!

Commercials were aimed at adults because they were the ones who bought "stuff." In fact, except for a few programs, like *The Pinky Lee Show* and *Howdy Doody*, there weren't a lot of shows just for kids until later in the 1950s.

It wasn't until whole Saturday mornings of cartoons came along in the late 1950s and early 1960s that kids started watching shows their parents didn't watch. And before long, advertisers realized that even though kids didn't have money to spend themselves, they could get their parents to buy "stuff" for them. So, for the first time in television history, commercials were aimed specifically at young people.

One program that everybody enjoyed in those days was *The Ed Sullivan Show*. It came on at 8:00 Sunday evenings and was what they called a "variety" show because it had so many different kinds of performers. In a single night, you might see a comedian, an opera star, a ballerina, a juggling act, and a ventriloquist.

In September 1956, Ed Sullivan booked a talented newcomer Ed first thought might not be suitable for family audiences. The way this young man moved his hips was upsetting to many adults.

And his music! The country and gospel songs he sang had a bluesy sound more like you'd find on Beale Street in the African American section of Memphis, where he was known to hang out in his spare time. You might have figured out by now that this young man was Elvis Presley. While he performed on Ed's show he played his rock 'n roll music and blew America away!

It wasn't the first time teens had liked a popular artist and a style of music their parents didn't like. But now that almost all teenagers were going to middle and high school, hanging out together afterward and on weekends, and watching TV, things were changing on a mass level.

TV shows like *American Bandstand,* which showed teenagers dancing to the latest hit songs, gave kids all over the country an instant update on music, dances, and teen fashions.

Rebel Without a Cause and *West Side Story* were movies *for* teens and *about* teens that set a trend for guys to wear ducktail haircuts, blue jeans, white t-shirts and black leather motorcycle jackets.

Most girls still expected to eventually get married and become mothers, so looking cute for guys was their goal. From ponytails and poodle skirts, they switched to black Capri pants and crisp, white shirts to copy Audrey Hepburn's look in the movie *Sabrina*. (Never heard of Audrey Hepburn? Ask your mom or grandma.)

Prior to this time, as long as everybody in the family needed to work to survive, parents and their kids had a lot in common. But now that teenagers were staying in school instead of working, they were becoming more and more *different* from their parents and *more like* one another.

By the time the first baby boomers reached their teens in 1959, they were already behaving very differently from their parents.

Rock-and-roll music, youthful fashion, drag racing, drive-ins, malt shops and high-school Greek societies were totally alien to the older generation.

A perfect storm was gaining momentum as preteens and teens became more and more unlike their parents and began to share **a growing collective mindset**, which went something like this:

*These are **our** kinds of clothes, not **your** kinds of clothes! This is **our** style of hair, not **your** style of hair! These are **our** toys/stuff, not **your** toys/stuff! This is **our** kind of music, not **your** kind of music! This is where **we** hang out, not where **you** hang out! This is **our** way of thinking, not **your** way of thinking!*

In addition, because they were staying in school longer, teens were learning more than their parents knew about a lot of things. Thus began the **"them-versus-us" Great Divide** between parents and teenagers that still survives today.

It was the end of the
"WE"
in families and the
beginning of the
"ME"
in families and teens.

Then, came the 1960s. **Oh boy, look out!**

The Sixties

Whole books have been written about the years from 1960 to 1969 because so much happened. It was a time of huge change, and young people played a major role in those changes. So did television, which was just beginning to show us the news as it was happening.

You know how you can remember exactly where you were and what you were doing when you learned about a major news event or a significant happening in the world? An event that you will never forget! Well, on November 22, 1963, teenagers across the country were sitting in class and heard their principal announce over the loud speaker that the President of the United States had just been killed.

Schools closed and, by the time kids got home, the details of John F. Kennedy's assassination were on every TV channel. Everyone was in a state of shock. How could this happen in the greatest country in the world? And to such a beloved President? To teens, it seemed that the adults – collectively referred to as "the establishment" – had made a huge mess of things.

Young people who didn't like what was going on began to reject society's norms. Some started a counter-culture that pushed the limits of just about everything.

"Proper" teen girls went from bouffant hairdos to very short or long straight hair, and flaunted their sexuality by wearing miniskirts and going without bras. Clean-cut guys grew beards and mustaches and let their hair get long enough to wear ponytails, which drove their parents' nuts.

African Americans of both sexes wore their hair in afros, and Motown's rhythm and blues sounds were playing on formerly all-white radio stations across the country.

The Civil Rights movement of the 1960s challenged anything that was "for whites only." Some people staged nonviolent sit-ins to protest discrimination against blacks. They also protested other things: unequal treatment of women and gays and the war in Vietnam. Often the protests turned violent, and people were injured and even killed.

Draft-eligible males who refused to go to a war they didn't believe in burned their draft cards and fled to Canada. Young people weren't defying *only* their parents, but all adults and society as well.

Without realizing it, the teens of the 1960s who saw the world in terms of **"us"** (youth) **versus "them"** (parents/adults) – **the Great Divide** – unknowingly intensified *The Great Teenage Myth.*

As a result, *The Great Teenage Myth* continued to strengthen through the 1970s and 1980s, which is when my peers and I unknowingly bought into it and perpetuated it. *The Great Teenage Myth* has continued to intensify and wreak havoc in young people's lives through the 1990s and now into the 21st Century.

I see you and other teenagers of today believing the *MYTH* and keeping it alive.

What you don't realize is how much it's hurting you!

Every day you unknowingly continue to believe and live the *MYTH*, you move farther and farther away from the very things you want in life: **Real Freedom, Real Independence, Real**

Personal Power, and **Fewer Hassles.**

That's right. The MYTH that you unknowingly believe with all your heart and mind is actually holding you back.

Okay, you have waited long enough.

I'm finally going to tell you *The Great Teenage Myth.*

Are you sure you're ready?

Because once you know this TRUTH, you will be forever changed. Even if you do nothing with this information, you will **never forget it!**

The
Great Teenage Myth
is your belief that
your parents are
"in control"
of you!

Yes, you read that correctly. In fact, let me repeat it again:

The Great Teenage Myth is your belief that your parents are "in control" of you!

You can put in parentheses next to "parents" any other authority figures you deal with: teachers, religious leaders, administrators, police, and society as a whole.

You might want to put down the book and think about the *MYTH* for a minute. Give yourself some time to get your mind wrapped around the idea. **It can seem pretty radical at first.**

In fact, I can already hear the argument going on in your head. "Wait a minute! They *are* in control. *They* set the rules. *They* don't let me do *this*; they don't let me do *that*."

In answer to your objections, I'd like to point out that there's a big difference between **rules** and **control.** In fact, it might help if you recognize that people of all ages – kids, teens and adults – are governed by rules and guidelines of some sort or another. And most rules are in our best interest, which is why we *choose* to obey them. For example, we abide by the rule to stop at red lights. Otherwise, we have made the *choice* to incur the potential consequences.

If you look at the definitions, **rules** and **guidelines** are similar. They are principles or regulations that govern conduct and action or provide guidance to appropriate behavior.

To be in **control**, however, is to hold power over people and events. The element of **choice** is what makes rules and guidelines different from control.

..... you have the opportunity to have an enormous influence and offer tremendous value to your children's lives. As a parent myself, I realized this TRUTH – *that I was not in control of my two sons* - the first day my wife and I put them on the school bus and waved goodbye as they were heading off to kindergarten. All we could hope for is that we had given them the proper tools and mindset to make good choices as they began their journey out in the world and learned to spread their wings.

It is crucial for parents to understand that the greatest challenge of parenting is that their child – their teenager – is continually developing and changing. This means that parenting must continually evolve and change.

The continual changes and development over the first 18 years of life are enormous! As parents, you must change and adapt your parenting strategies and efforts or you will experience a disconnect with your children as they grow!

Set simple, yet firm, limits and guidelines, but continually review, reevaluate and readjust them as needed. Discuss and teach morals and values, but know your teenagers will have to think through and craft them on their own.

You must allow your teenagers to spread their wings and fly on their own, knowing that they will want to fly farther and farther. You must let go and allow them to make their own mistakes, for life at times can be the best teacher of all.

Love them for who they are at that moment and honor their uniqueness, for they are each special and are meant to do amazing things in their life.

Know it is only them – individually – who can come to terms with *The Great Teenage Myth* and how it can be harmful, destructive and limiting to their life.

When you believe in, and live, *The Great Teenage Myth!*

Believing and living the *MYTH* that your parents are "in control" actually confines and restrains your freedom like a prisoner! What you really believe is that you have no power. "They" have it all. This gives you someone else to blame when things don't turn out the way you want. "It's all *their* fault, not *mine.*" "If it weren't for *them, I* could do/be this." "*I'm* not responsible, because *they* are responsible!"

As long as you can place the blame on others, you can avoid being responsible for yourself. But once you SHATTER the *MYTH* and recognize that your parents are not in control, that they only set guidelines and rules attempting to teach you morals and values they believe are in your best interest (even if they are wrong), the next logical question is: *Who IS in control?*

Brace yourself for the answer…

YOU ARE! That's right. **YOU. YES – YOU ARE IN CONTROL OF YOU!**

YOU ALWAYS HAVE BEEN AND ALWAYS WILL BE!

Your parents set rules and guidelines, which you **choose** to obey or **choose** not to obey because **YOU ARE IN CONTROL!** You know what will happen if you don't follow the rules. Therefore, if you **choose** to break them, it means you're willing to accept the negative consequences. Why? Because **YOU ARE IN CONTROL!**

But wait! If you're in control, then …

Who is responsible?

Yes, it's **YOU!**

Of course, that means that, when you "screw up" by making an "irresponsible choice," you have made your proverbial "bed to lie in." Thus, it is your **choice** to accept the full blame.

But you also get all the credit, all the pleasure, and all the sense of accomplishment and cool results for every responsible choice you make. You truly can, and do, create your own FREEDOM and SUCCESS.

When it comes to your acceptance or lack of acceptance of the TRUTH of *The Great Teenage Myth*, you will find that you are hanging out in one of three camps.

Which camp are you in?

<u>Camp #1 - A Prisoner</u>

You DO NOT Believe

The Great Teenage Myth Exists

After reading *The Great Teenage Myth*, you still don't believe it's true. For whatever reasons, you just accept and believe the idea –

the paradigm – that your parents are "in control."

You also believe that other people (teachers, administrators, coaches, the police, bosses, etc.), or structures (schools, governments, society) are "in control." So be it … for now anyway. But what you cannot deny is that you have made a **choice** not to accept *The Great Teenage Myth* as true. Therefore, you cannot deny that you indeed have the power to **choose** – to make **choices** in, and for, your life.

Understand, you make hundreds of **choices** each and every day. **Choices** about the thoughts you have, **choices** that result in your behaviors that create your results, **choices** about the feelings you experience, and **choices** about how you perceive yourself, others and the world.

If this is the camp you're currently hanging out in, well, I would bet money (if I was a gambler) that you DO NOT EXPERIENCE in your life all the **Real Freedom, Real Independence,** and **Real Personal Power** you desire deep down inside. You also experience a lot of **Hassles** in your life!

You blame others, you blame situations, you blame circumstances, and you blame the world for what happens to you and for what *is happening*, or *not happening*, in your life. In other words, you blame the world for the results <u>you created</u> by ***your choices***. You experience yourself as being a victim. You have reoccurring thoughts of "poor me." You are not experiencing a life of growth and abundance that is your birthright, the one you are entitled to and deserve.

You are truly shackled like a prisoner!

<u>Camp #2</u>
Pseudo-Freedom

If, after reading *The Great Teenage Myth*, you have any of these thoughts: *"Yeah, I know my parents (teachers, administrators, the police, society, etc.) are not in control of ME!"* Or *"They can't tell*

ME *what to do, or what to think!"* Or *"You're not the boss of ME, I am the boss of ME!"* Or something like the above, you're in Camp #2.

Pseudo means false, fake, not real. So you do in fact have the experience of **freedom**, **independence** and **personal power**, but know it is nothing more than a pseudo-freedom, a pseudo-independence and a pseudo-personal power. You live a false and fake experience of what you truly desire and need.

Again, what you cannot deny is that you have made a **choice** not to accept *The Great Teenage Myth* as true. Therefore, you cannot deny that you indeed have the power to **choose** – to make **choices** in, and for, your life.

Again understand that you make hundreds of **choices** each and every day. **Choices** about the thoughts you have, **choices** that result in your behaviors and your behaviors create your results, **"choices"** about the feelings you experience, **"choices"** on how you perceive yourself, how you perceive others and how you perceive the world.

If this is the camp you're currently hanging out in, well, I would again bet money (if I was a gambler, and I am not) that you do not experience in your life all of the **Real Freedom, Real Independence** and **Real Personal Power** you desire deep down inside. I also know that you experience a lot of **Hassles** in your life!

You pride yourself on being rebellious, defiant, oppositional, "your own man" or "your own woman" and you look for shortcuts in, and for, your life. You experience the constant feelings of anger, confusion and frustration. You blame others and external circumstances for your results but, instead of playing the "poor me" card you have **chosen** to rise up against the perceived injustices done to you with an angry, frustrated, defiant and rebellious attitude and mindset.

You guard yourself against the world, at times **choosing** to strike back, or "get even," and your attitude is usually one of resistance.

You are no longer shackled (which actually is a few steps closer to a freer, more independent and more prosperous life), but you still are a prisoner. Your tendency is to take from life, because **you believe you are owed something and are due.**

You are closer, but not yet truly free …

<u>Camp #3 True Freedom</u>

You Have Shattered

The Great Teenage Myth

The Great Teenage Myth, confirms for you what you already know and live: that YOU are indeed responsible for you, you are the captain of your own ship, therefore you experience **Real Freedom, Real Independence, Real Personal Power,** and **Fewer Hassles** in **your life!**

Whether you are the small percentage of youth who just "get it" – *that you are responsible for the choices you make and the results you get in your life* — or you have evolved your thinking and become aware of your own power, and thus taken responsible control of your life through a conscious effort – know that you have arrived and understand that no one can "rain on your parade!"

You have arrived and understand that your choices create your results!

You have arrived and understand that you can use your mind and imagination to create the life you desire!

You have arrived and understand that challenges are only opportunities that bring you closer to your dreams and goals!

You have arrived and understand that no one can influence your feelings and your attitude but you!

You have arrived and understand that your time is your most valuable asset and, through focus and intention, can leverage your time to create the results you desire!

You have arrived and understand that you can use the power of gratitude and forgiveness in your life!

You have arrived and understand that you are a unique champion whose birthright is happiness, success and achievement!

- You are truly FREE.
- You are truly INDEPENDENT.
- You are truly connected with your PERSONAL POWER.
- You experience FEW HASSLES.

Paradigms

First, you need to recognize that shattering *The Great Teenage Myth* requires a paradigm shift. A *paradigm* is a set of assumptions that make up the way we view reality. Remember the part about changing your perceptions, seeing and experiencing the box differently (a NEW understanding) and thinking "outside the box"? Let me give you two examples of paradigm shifts that you may already know.

You remember Christopher Columbus? When he was alive, most everyone believed that the world was flat, and they believed that, if they walked far enough, they would fall right off the edge of the world.

Christopher Columbus had a notion that maybe the world wasn't flat after all. So, he went to the Queen for support (he was actually a fur trader). He wanted to sail the seas to the West, to find a quicker path to the East (this would make the fur trading more profitable), and prove that the world wasn't flat. And, with the Queen's help, that's just what he did.

He not only found that the world wasn't flat; he discovered a new land, which shook the world at that time to its very foundations.

For the majority of people who thought the world was flat, it was almost as if they were caged – a "prisoner" by *their own thinking*. It was a paradigm that **limited** them. "Walk too far, and you'll fall off the edge" created an unnecessary fear of going anywhere. Once Christopher Columbus shattered that *MYTH*, people could, and did, travel to whole new lands, and **many, many new opportunities resulted.**

Those of us who live in America benefit directly every day from the vision and courage of Christopher Columbus. Think how different your life would be today without that paradigm shift!

Another example of a limiting paradigm is the concept that the Earth revolves around the sun. Today we accept this as a TRUTH but, less than 400 years ago, most people believed the sun and all the planets revolved around the Earth. When Galileo published papers in the early 1600s stating what he had observed through his telescope, he was charged with the crime of heresy for opposing the teachings of the Church, the "belief", of that time. The normal penalty for heresy was death, but Galileo was "lucky" because he was sentenced to life imprisonment rather than put to death.

It was very difficult for the people of that time to accept that Galileo was right. The truth didn't match their paradigm, their "belief", that the Earth was the center of the universe.

In order for a paradigm shift to occur, people have to abandon an idea they have always accepted as TRUTH. That's not easy to do!

Shattering *The Great Teenage Myth* may not be easy either, because it too is a paradigm – a belief. Shattering this *MYTH* requires shifting something you've believed your whole life. So give yourself a break and know this could take some time, but the rewards you will gain in your life will be spectacular!

Up to this point, you have believed *The Great Teenage Myth* through no fault of your own. But now that you ***know*** it's a *MYTH* and have an understanding of how *this MYTH* came to be and how it restricts you, you're left with a **choice**.

What choice will you make going forward as you create your life day after day?

You now KNOW that there is no way you can EVER experience **Real Freedom, Real Independence, Real Personal Power** and **Fewer Hassles** unless you shatter *The Great Teenage Myth* and take responsibility for your thoughts, your feelings and your actions.

Just remember ...
YOU are in control!

Sooooo, what can you do from this point forward?

Know that **Real Freedom, Real Independence, Real Personal Power,** and **Fewer Hassles** exist all around you if you will only step forward and claim these experiences that are meant for you!

There are specific ideas and strategies you can begin to embrace and leverage in, and for, your life whenever you decide to do so!

There is no mystery or magic to this fact although, when you decide to step forward, you will experience your life as magical!

All that is needed is the correct mindset, a willingness to take correct action, and the willingness to "let go" of the "old" (your past) as you move forward through each moment and each day.

Awaken to the TRUTH: In this very moment you are creating your future for better or for worse. Life is not stagnant; life is in constant flow and motion. The question truly is: *Will you take advantage of your opportunities and begin to leverage your potential today?* Or will you wait for another day, another week, another month or another year? Or will you never take advantage of your opportunities and potential at all? That would be sad.

It really is all up to you! It always has been and it always will be up to you!

What is your choice?

Do you choose to step forward?

Beyond The Great Teenage Myth

*1) **YOU HAVE BEEN GIVEN A GIFT – OPEN IT!*** Human beings are unique creatures. You have been bestowed with the ability to THINK. You are able to THINK ideas and consider ideas with the ability to roll them around in your mind to determine if the *idea* can or cannot be of value to you and your life.

It has been nothing more, or nothing less, than ideas that have created the world we live in. Single ideas have changed the world throughout history. A single idea has changed countless lives forever.

Are you going to open your gift and experiment with it and use it — or not?

2) ***YOUR GIFT OF IMAGINATION!*** You not only have been given the gift to THINK, you have been given the gift of IMAGINATION. You can use your mind to imagine anything you want; you can create picture after picture on the canvas of your mind. Know that anything anybody has *accomplished* in their life, or anything anybody has *created* in their life, was first an image in their mind.

All the "stuff" you see in the world was first an image in someone's mind. Any accomplishment – playing a musical instrument, developing sport skills, becoming a good student, learning to drive, flying a plane (the list could go on and on) – were first a desired image in someone's mind.

Never, EVER underestimate or forget the power of your imagination!

3) ***YOU ARE IN CONTROL!*** Whether you accept this or not, it is a TRUTH. Somewhere deep inside of you, if you listen closely, you will resonate with the TRUTH that **you are in control**. This is not a question of *"is this true or not true,"* the question is if and when you will embrace this TRUTH.

When, you make the **choice** to embrace and harness your ability to control your life, you will be able to use and leverage your incredible potential and your personal power.

*4) **THE POWER OF CHOICE!*** At the very core of your being, at every moment in your life, you have the ability to make a **choice.** If you really consider the TRUTH of this, you will realize you are making **choices** all the time:

The **choice** to listen or not.
The **choice** to study or not.
The **choice** of what you will eat or not.
The **choice** to do or not do.
The **choice** to be a happy person or not .
The **choice** to _____ .

You fill in the blank(s).

It does not matter one bit how pleasant or unpleasant your external circumstances are, it does not matter one bit how another person is treating you, it does not matter if someone says words of kindness or ugliness to you – you have the power to **choose** your thoughts and attitudes. No one, no circumstance, can determine your feelings. It is always your **choice** to decide your thoughts, your attitude, your actions and reactions and how you are going to feel.

5) **YOU INVEST YOUR TIME!** You have exactly 168 hours in your week, just like everyone else has 168. I call this an "equal opportunity week." You don't "spend" your time, you "invest" your time!

How you invest your time will determine the results you get in your life. This is a TRUTH for every person who has ever walked this amazing planet, a TRUTH for every person who is now walking on this amazing planet, and a TRUTH for everyone who will come to walk on this amazing planet. If you reflect on your past results, both positive and negative, you will understand the TRUTH of this fact.

What follows are a few aspects regarding teen life for you to think about and to consider how you will invest your time today and going forward:

5a) **Invest to become a successful student.** I don't necessarily mean being an A student, although being an A/B student is most likely achievable by the majority. The line between success and failure for most students is paper thin. You are at school for approximately 40 hours a week. Why not use the time wisely and to your advantage?

How well are you investing your focus and action during your school day?

How well are you investing your six plus hours at home after school?

5b) **Invest in your family relationships.** This takes a willingness and openness by both you and your parents. But you can only control you! Consider …

Kind words go a long way!

Pitching in for 5, 10, 15 minutes a day around the house is being a team player!

Asking your parents how their day has been, knowing they have ups and downs as well and that their life can be hectic just like yours!

That your parents are doing the best they can (everyone is doing the best they can), no matter how good or not so good they may be doing at that time!

That many teens who "did not like their parents" at age 10, 12, 15 or 18, like, admire and thank them for their efforts when they are older. For your own good get over it sooner rather than later!

5c) **Invest in healthy peer relationships.** Be careful of the "herd mentality" alive in the teenage community, especially those of a negative nature: "school stinks," "the teachers are …," "parents …," "doing drugs won't hurt you."

Know that walking away from the herd for a good reason does not mean you have to leave the herd for good. Also know, that if you must walk away from a herd that is making harmful choices, you most likely will find a herd that is making better choices.

Our world needs young people to create a more responsible, supportive and respectful herd for themselves, for each other, for today and for the future.

5d) Invest in YOU, not the courts or the lawyers. Choose to behave in ways that keep you out of legal troubles. These types of results in your life only restrict and shrink your freedom. Legal incidents usually cost money (sometimes a lot of money) that can be used for other opportunities and things – maybe even things for you: a car, new clothes, electronics, college, etc.

5e) Invest in taking care of your body and mind. This gets into a reality and challenge that many young people face: the question of experimenting with alcohol and drugs. No matter how fun or enjoyable the high may be, know that the fun is ALWAYS short-lived and has a price attached to it!

Experimentation is short-lived, then "use" begins and almost always increases over time. If you are heading down this path, know that difficulties, hard times, destruction, loss, and a host of other problems are not far away.

Exercise and be active in your life! Your body is the vehicle that connects you to this earth. Your mind is a powerful tool that should be strengthened and should be leveraged in this abundant and opportunistic world we live in.

5f) Invest some energy to create cash flow. If you are old enough to work and have the ability, time and desire to work, you can begin to generate money in your life. It's cool and valuable to have a steady cash flow in your life, and it's even cooler when you are the one creating it.

Three ways to <u>legally</u> create and generate cash as a teen:

1) Go to work for a company (fast food, grocery store, retail store, etc.).

2) Neighborhood jobs (mowing lawns, washing cars, raking leaves, shoveling snow, baby/pet sitting).

3) Start and build a company (many teens and young adults have taken this path).

5g) **Invest in you, you are a Leader.** At the minimum, lead your own life successfully, for we ALL are the Leader(s) of our lives.

By having **H**ope (your vision and goals), nurturing your hope with **I**nspiration (the passion, effort and action in your life), and always **P**ersevering through the challenging times, you will progress farther down the path and closer to your goal. As a result, you will create wonderful and great things for yourself.

If you add the **H**, the **I** and the **P** to Leaders, you get LEADERSHIP!

Our world does not need any more followers! Our world needs each of us to be the Leader of our own life as we stand side by side with each other!

6) **YOUR STORY IS NOT WHO YOU ARE TODAY!** Every moment and experience you have had prior to this moment is only a memory – it's YOUR STORY. **It is not who you are now!**

In this moment, you have the opportunity to take control of your life and use the *wonderful gifts* you have been bestowed. You have the gift and the ability to use your mind and THINK, the gift and the ability to use your IMAGINATION to create, the gift and the ability to harness your personal power to make valuable **choices**, to direct your life toward your dreams, and to create happiness and success.

Your story is meant only for you to learn from and to guide you more effectively TODAY; it's not meant for you to hang on to, thus shackling you to your past each day.

7) **YOU ARE A CHAMPION!** You are AMAZING! You are SPECIAL! You are UNIQUE! You are WONDERFUL! You have vast, vast amounts of UNLIMITED POTENTIAL just waiting and wanting to emerge and express itself through you and your life.

In all of human history, there has never been another you! In all of the future history to come, there will **NEVER, EVER BE ANOTHER YOU!**

You are one of a kind and this is your time! You are meant to shine!

NEVER FORGET THIS!

YOUR NEW BEGINNING

One and Only You

Every single blade of grass,
And every flake of snow –
Is just a wee bit different ...
There's no two alike you know.

From something small,
Like grains of sand,
All were made with THIS in mind:
To be just what they are!

How foolish then, to imitate –
How useless to pretend!
Since each of us comes from a MIND
Whose ideas never end.

There'll only be just ONE of ME
To show what I can do –
And you should likewise feel very proud,
There's only ONE of YOU.

That is where it all starts
With you, a wonderful unlimited human being.

James T. Moore

Author's Note

Now that I have shared with you *The Great Teenage Myth*, I must give you a little background about how I discovered it.

I have been working for the last 20 years as a licensed counselor, professional speaker, consultant and trainer. During my professional career, I have worked with, and spoken to, thousands of preteens, teenagers, young adults, college students, collegiate and professional athletes, parents, educators, and colleagues.

This has led to a great understanding of what makes preteens, teenagers, and young adults successful, and what blocks them from having the inherent success they desire and are meant to have in their lives.

During my professional career, I have been taught more by the people I have had the privilege of working with than the ideas and teaching I have tried to share and offer to others. This is just another example that confirms a point I make in *The Great Teenage Myth:* that life is TRULY about the "WE" and not about the "ME." For the learning I have received, I am humbly grateful.

If it weren't for the thousands of people I have worked with, *The Great Teenage Myth* probably never could have been discovered.

I also am a former teenager myself, with a mother and a father just like everyone else. I now am a father, *a parent*, of two wonderful boys who are growing into young men. Therefore, *The Great Teenage Myth* was not only discovered through my professional work, but also through my personal experience of living and growing up human.

Over the years, the reactions from the countless preteens, teens, young adults and parents after I have shared with them *The Great Teenage Myth* confirms its TRUTH. Actually, it is a TRUTH wrapped in our historical human history story and, as I share it with others, it has both inspired and awakened the human mind and human spirit..

I believe that it *speaks to* the part in all of us that TRULY knows we are responsible for our choices, actions and behaviors.

More importantly, it is the CHAMPION inside each of us that desires to emerge and excel *through us* that knows that *The Great Teenage Myth* is truly a lie that we have unknowingly believed and that it ultimately keeps us trapped, keeping us a prisoner.

Understanding *The Great Teenage Myth* and shattering this *MYTH* in our life is foundational for each of us – individually and collectively!

"Foundational" meaning that, by shattering the *MYTH* and taking responsibility for our choices and actions, we then have a strong foundation to create, build and grow success in all areas in our lives. You may want to reread *The Great Teenage Myth* many times to TRULY and DEEPLY digest it, and to get a full understanding of it.

I am honored that you are here and have chosen to read *The Great Teenage Myth,* and I wish for you the strength and courage to shatter this *MYTH* you may be living today.

All the best to you!

Respectfully,
Joseph P. Gandolfo
2009

Acknowledgements

Countless individuals are to thank for this book coming to be. The thousands of young people, parents and educators I have had the privilege to work with over the years. Each one of you is a champion!

To all of my family, personal friends and many professional friends, including many in the National Speakers Association - all of you offered me your ideas, your heart and your support! Thank You!

To name a few: my wife Tonya, my sons Duncan and Cole, my mother, my father and my Italian family. Wayne, Mike B., Smitty, Dan Thurmon, Dr. Anne Richards, Shirley Garrett, David Ryback, Rob Skinner, Jean Houston Shore, Marc LeBlanc, Tom Kell and Larry Manno. You have all meant more to my life journey than you will ever know. Thank You!

To Bonnie, Melanie and Kay, whose researching, writing and editing expertise has allowed this work to come alive in this world. Thank You!

To Morgan James Publishing, who has extended an opportunity and support to make this book available to the world. Thank You!

I love all of you!

Joe Gandolfo

Additional Programs
and Products
to help You Realize
Your Potential ...

Success Coaching, Life Coaching Programs

The power lies within each of us to THINK, to make responsible CHOICES, and to CREATE and direct our lives toward SUCCESSFUL RESULTS!

All-Star School Performance
For many students, the line between academic success and academic struggle is paper thin. This highly focused school performance program offers students a proven structure and fresh strategies which will allow them to achieve academic success within one (1) semester.

Drugs & Alcohol: The "Cat's Out of the Bag"
For a family, when IT "comes to light" that their son or daughter has been experimenting and using drugs and/or alcohol, the "playing field" changes forever. This highly structured program will address the activity of drug & alcohol use, it offers a focused plan to support efforts towards non-use and will support the family in its efforts to rebuild trust.

Growing Friendships: A Social Skills Program
During the pre-teen and teen years, having friendships and being part of one's "peer community" becomes a strong desire in each young person. Navigating the world of friendships can be a "difficult process", but it does not have to be. Social skills are learnable skills and growing positive friendships is achievable by all.

Think & Grow _____ *: Success Begins With You!*

You have the power to THINK, to CHOOSE and to CREATE your own SUCCESS. This program focuses on Personal Development and The Laws of Success. There are particular structures and strategies which when understood and lived, almost guarantees one's life will move toward success, achievement and prosperity. Specifically, teaching how to ignite one's imagination, how to harness and focus one's thinking, and how to leverage the power of "choice" and take action to overcome challenges, and seize the abundant opportunities for growth.

Ready for Graduation & The Real World (seniors only)

When a senior walks thru their school doors on the "first day" of their senior year, the notion that high school is coming to an end hits them "smack on the head". The next 18 months of their life is in a "state of transition" as they determine what they are "going to do with the rest of their life". This program focuses on making sure the senior graduates and has developed a plan for the next phase of their life.

... wait, there is more!

Invite Joe to speak at your next event!

Many of today's pre-teens, teenagers and young adults are LOST! Many of today's parents are confused and struggle trying to connect to have a positive impact on their children! Educators are searching for fresh ideas and strategies so they can influence positive growth in the students they serve! Are you searching for FRESH HOPE? Are you looking for a way to REKINDLE YOUR INSPIRATION? Do you need to strengthen your WILL TO PERSERVERE? Are you ready to make positive life changes that bring success, achievement and happiness? If so, **your event needs Joe!**

To check availability for coaching, speaking, consulting or training
contact us at 678-640-000 or visit www.JosephGandolfo.com

Joseph P. Gandolfo, M.A, LPC

Joe is a conveyor of powerful ideas and principles that change lives. He is on a mission to champion the greatest commodity in today's world - our youth, teenagers and young adults, as well as to rally, strengthen and energize the adults - parents, educators, health professionals and organizations - who work with and care about our young people.

For nearly 20 years, Joe has engaged firsthand the human experience as a licensed counselor. He has coached, counseled and spoken to thousands of individuals and groups including youth, teenagers, collegiate student-athletes, professional athletes, adults, parents, educators, public and private schools, organizations and associations.

Joe firmly believes that there is structure to success, and his programs lead young people to reach their greatest potential. As a professional speaker, success coach, seminar leader, motivational counselor and author, Joe challenges preteens, teens and young adults to make effective decisions and build their lives in positive ways. He also provides parents, educators and health professionals with the insight, ideas and information they need to understand, communicate with and support young people.

Joe is the CEO and President of Joseph Gandolfo International, Inc., a professional speaking, training, success coaching and consulting organization.

Joe served as a consultant with the Homer Rice Center for Sports Performance at Georgia Tech (2000 -2007), and as an adjunct professor for both Georgia Tech (1996 - 2000) and Georgia State University (2006). His clients have included the Georgia Tech Athletic Association, Rockdale County Schools, The Lovett School, Cobb County Schools, SAPA, Cobb Teen Leadership, YMCA, Childcare Resource Network, Georgia Tech, University of Clemson, Georgia State University, University of West Georgia, PGA of America, The National Association of Golf Coaches and Educators, Milwaukee Brewers, Coca-Cola, SouthCoast Hospitals, Owens-Corning and MPI Georgia Chapter.

To Contact Joseph Gandolfo International

Call:	**678-640-0000**
Email:	**joe@JosephGandolfo.com**
Website:	**www.JosephGandolfo.com**
Write:	**1000 Johnson Ferry Road**
	Suite B-200
	Marietta, Georgia 30068
	USA

FREE eBook BONUS

One Powerful Idea

The
Great Teenage Myth

909 More Incredible Ideas for YOU!

303 Solutions for
Accomplishing More in Less Time - eBook

303 Solutions for
Dropping Stress and Finding Balance - eBook

303 Solutions for
Developing the Leader in You – eBook

DOWNLOAD FOR FREE the 3 eBooks @

**www.TheGreatestTeenageMythInTheWorld.com/
TGTMBookBonus**

And **REMEMBER – tell a friend about this book!**

FREE AUDIO PODCASTS

Teen Success Radio is a free motivational and inspirational audio podcast for pre-teens, teens and young adults.

You may download and listen by going to iTunes and typing in the search "Teen Success Radio" or by using this link:

http://joegandolfo.hipcast.com/rss/teen_success_radio.xml

That Elusive Parenting Manual is a free audio podcast for parents who find raising their children challenging at best and frustrating at worst. TEPM offers parents ideas, strategies and a fresh perspective on the art of parenting.

You may download and listen by going to iTunes and typing in the search "That Elusive Parenting Manual" or by using this link:

http://joegandolfo.hipcast.com/rss/that_elusive_parenting_manual.xml

Teens Success Radio and *That Elusive Parenting Manual*
is hosted and produced by Joe Gandolfo and the World Teen Network.
www.JosephGandolfo.com

BUY A SHARE OF THE FUTURE IN YOUR COMMUNITY

These certificates make great holiday, graduation and birthday gifts that can be personalized with the recipient's name. The cost of one S.H.A.R.E. or one square foot is $54.17. The personalized certificate is suitable for framing and will state the number of shares purchased and the amount of each share, as well as the recipient's name. The home that you participate in "building" will last for many years and will continue to grow in value.

Here is a sample SHARE certificate:

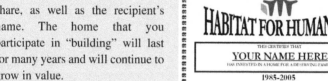

HABITAT FOR HUMANITY

THIS CERTIFIES THAT

YOUR NAME HERE

HAS INVESTED IN A HOME FOR A DESERVING FAMILY

1985-2005

TWENTY YEARS OF BUILDING FUTURES IN OUR COMMUNITY ONE HOME AT A TIME

1200 SQUARE FOOT HOUSE @ $65,000 = $54.17 PER SQUARE FOOT
This certificate represents a tax deductible donation. It has no cash value.

YES, I WOULD LIKE TO HELP!

I support the work that Habitat for Humanity does and I want to be part of the excitement! As a donor, I will receive periodic updates on your construction activities but, more importantly, I know my gift will help a family in our community realize the dream of homeownership. **I would like to SHARE in your efforts against substandard housing in my community!** *(Please print below)*

PLEASE SEND ME _____ SHARES at $54.17 EACH = $ $_____

In Honor Of: _____

Occasion: (Circle One)   HOLIDAY   BIRTHDAY   ANNIVERSARY

OTHER: _____

Address of Recipient: _____

Gift From: _____ *Donor Address:* _____

Donor Email: _____

I AM ENCLOSING A CHECK FOR $ $_____ PAYABLE TO HABITAT FOR HUMANITY <u>OR</u> PLEASE CHARGE MY VISA OR MASTERCARD *(CIRCLE ONE)*

Card Number _____ Expiration Date: _____

Name as it appears on Credit Card _____ Charge Amount $ _____

Signature _____

Billing Address _____

Telephone # Day _____ Eve _____

PLEASE NOTE: Your contribution is tax-deductible to the fullest extent allowed by law.
Habitat for Humanity • P.O. Box 1443 • Newport News, VA 23601 • 757-596-5553
www.HelpHabitatforHumanity.org